*To my parents, for my wonderful childhood memories, and their love and support through the years ~* Joni
*To my lil' Liggie, may there be many magical moments in your life, filled with adventure and love ~* Laura

Copyright © 2014 by Laura Sidsworth
Cover Painting © 2014 Joni Anttila
Internal Paintings © 2014 Joni Anttila
All Rights Reserved.
No part of this book may be reproduced in any form, or by any
electronic or mechanical systems; including photocopying, recording,
or any information storage retrieval system—except in the case of brief
quotations embedded in critical articles or reviews—without explicit
permission in writing from the author and artist.
Published by Animal Valley Artists
Library of Congress Control Number: 2014908899
ISBN-13: 978-0991261956
Printed in U.S.A.
For hardback orders, prints & calendars, visit: www.thetreehousetreasury.com

SPECIAL THANKS TO
**Radiator Media** *and* **Zamo Creative**

# The TREEHOUSE TREASURY

PAINTINGS BY
Joni Anttila

WRITTEN BY
Laura Sidsworth

# The Treehouse

A wind's gentle breeze
*rustles*
green leafy leaves
Branches creak bit by bit
but roots are *deep*...
*deeper,* **deep.**
A lush leafy canopy
*shelters*
animals you can
and cannot see
On a *sunny* day...
or under *rainy* skies -
a pleasant house the tree provides!

# Building

Hammers, saws, and coveralls,
ladders, wood, and building walls.
Inside and outside
work all anew -
framing and windows
let streaming sun through.
Shingles in bundles
jammed all in a pack
get nailed to the roof
with a tap, tap, and tap.
Painting and window boxes
a flowerpot or two -
workers work hard so many days through!

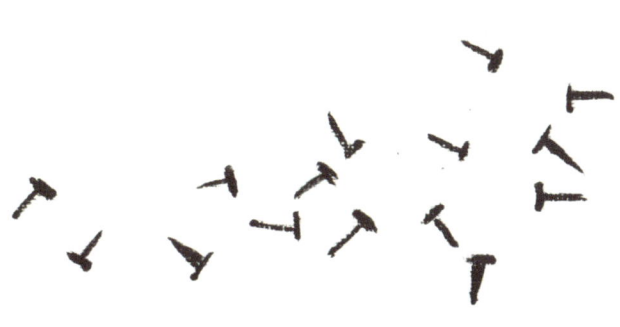

# Valentine's

Hearts
cut out of love
wrapped in lace
with tender care
painted red
that dare to say
I love you first!
So there, so there!

# Hiking

*Alone* or with friends
**deep** in the woods
or *high* in the hills
across desert floors
or great rocky canyons -
*hiking is liking*
*what nature can show.*
Blue skies delight
with a sun that's on fire
clouds flit above
some *high*, and some *higher*.
Snow in the mountains
blue lakes below
walking and walking -
then *walking* some more.

Around boulders and rocks
around many a bend -
come tons of surprises
*all* without end....
Pine trees and oaks
blossoms and bees
a feather or leaf
*float* down on a breeze.
Breathing, *breathing*...
fresh air so sweet
the smell of the earth
so **deep** under feet -
that are walking, *just walking*...
to nature's own beat.

Nature awakens!
Bright colors wake from dark dreams -
warm, fun days are here!

# A Day at the Lake

**A**
hot summer
**day**
friends meet
**at**
a blue oasis, sparkling in
**the**
sunshine...
swimmers and boats
float on ripples and waves
atop the shimmering
**lake.**

# Fishing with Papa

Early yawns - it's dawn.
Cool air *lingers* upon **darkened** lake.
Shadows *lurk* beneath
water wetly lapping at
the wooden feet of the pier.
Echoing sounds
of *plink* and *plunk*
splash against aluminum boats
farther off - afloat.
Wooden hulls splash differently,
sounds of *dink* and *dunk*
upon gently rocking boats.

The sun slowly rises,
*warming* hearts to its charms.
Light pinks and orange
*light* the way to brilliant day....
Breaths are held and caught
by a fishing line cast out -
*both* are let out, and brought in again....
Responding circles on the water's surface
*ripple* out and *about*.
Peaceful and quiet is this day at the lake
but for small splashing sounds
*plink* and *plunk*, and *dink* and *dunk*
an occasional gasp - and small shout
with the *jump* and a **splish**...
of a fish caught at last,
by someone's best cast.

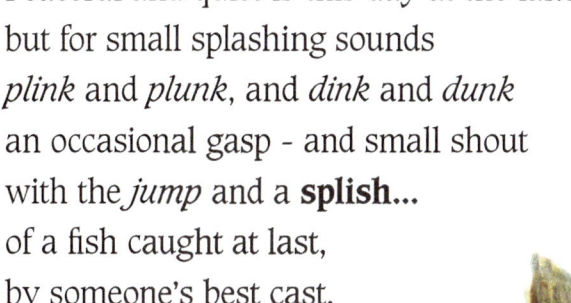

# A Day at the Beach

A sunny, bunny
day at the beach...
the sky
so high
and bright, and blue!
The ocean splashing, crashing through -
sandcastles safer
up on the beach
are built shaping sand,
no easy feat.
Beach blankets and buckets
sand shovels and ball -
or just laying back,
enjoying it all...
ah, a sunny bunny
day at the beach!

# The Lemonade Stand

It's hot and dusty.
I'm tired and thirsty.
I'm done playing and I'm a little bored, too.
Mom has an idea,
"Make a lemonade stand!"
First, I pick fresh lemons
from our backyard tree.
Next, I decide an old crate
would make a great table.
Our front yard will be my store!
A pretty pitcher of water
to squeeze the lemon juice into
and cups are all I need.
I taste...oh, sour face I make!
Mom laughs and hands me the sugar bowl.
A few spoonfuls and now the lemonade is done!
It's delicious!
I'm not thirsty anymore, and neither are
my neighbors!
Mmm...juicy fresh lemonade for sale!

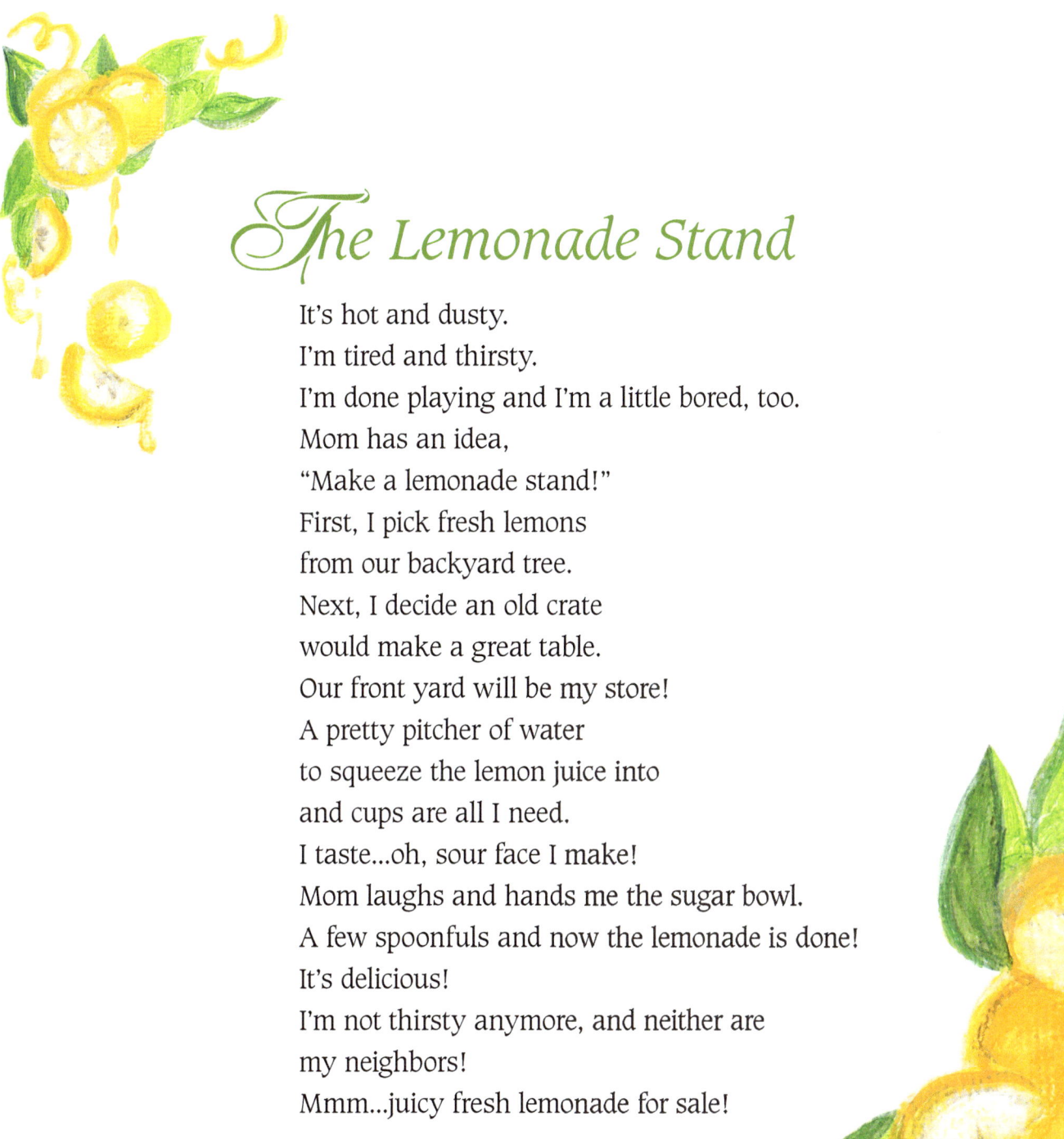

# Farmers' Market

From the ground up
anything anyone eats,
vegetables, fruits, or grain
is grown by farmers -
who plant seeds and saplings—
water, fertilize, watch, and wait....
The seeds, under sunny skies
sprout to seedlings that grow
to plants, bushes, vines, and trees
and...after a time in the growing season -
usually spring to fall,
comes a harvesting so bountiful,
one can hardly believe it all!
A farmers' market is an outdoor store,
selling everything fresh -
spring, summer, and fall.

# Camping

The night **deepens** darkly
stars *twinkle* bright...
an owl sits perched
amidst dusky twilight.
The forest air *fresh*
with the smell of tall pines
it is time to unwind...
*unpack* all of one's mind.
The tinder is set
the fire grows higher,
sitting and snacking...
the flames do *inspire*
stories and songs
a shared sing-along
coyotes howl near—
and *all* turn to hear.
The night **deepens** darkly
stars *twinkle* bright...
it is time to lie down,
and to say our goodnights!

# Dress-up

Dress-up is fun
any ol' time
I can wear yours
and you can wear mine.
Purses and clutches
a box of old clothes
flowers and hats
we strike such a pose!
In mama's high heels
and dresses too long
we preen and pretend
to royalty we belong!

# Halloween

Bats on the wing
cats on the prowl
coyotes and wolves
yip, yap, and howl.
Halloween treats
wait for kids in costume
"Trick or treat" are the words
one must use to consume.
A "Thank you," a twirl
a bow, and repeat
there is nothing as fine
as a Halloween treat.

# Mama Cat in the Kitchen

Mama's in the kitchen
the batter's in her bowl
she adds molasses, eggs, and flour
and lets us spoon and swirl.
The oven's set to baking
the cookies come out done -
the gingerbread is set to cool...
and brother snags just one!

# Wintertime

A cold cloudy day
rain freezes in the grey sky
white snow softly falls.

It snowed overnight!
My mom says there is enough
to build a snowman!

# A Visit with Santa

Every year as Christmas draws near
I am dressed in my best
to face my old fear -
Santa!
Candy cane in hand, he's dressed all in red
"Have you been good?" I hear in my head.
I think and I thought
of the times I was not
and then I am there -
with Santa!
I am shy, but stand tall
and finally tell all -
to jolly ol' Santa!

# Skiing

Snow softly falling
wind in our hair
the chair lifts us
higher, *higher*... into the air.
Skis on our feet
poles in our hand
*reaching* the peak -
with a **jump** we must land.
Then gliding, *gliding*...
over glistening white snow
a feeling of freedom -
a **rush**... and a *glow!*

# Family Time

In the evening
after school, work, dinner,
dishes, homework, baths,
and brushing our teeth -
it is family time.
We snuggle near
to hear stories of
dragons and Princes
castles and Princesses
fairytales and scary tales.
Grandma knits
and papa reads.
The clock gently
tick-tocks out the minutes…
till it's time for bed.

# Nighttime

Hushed, *hushed* becomes the day.
Dark, *dark* becomes the night.
The moon (so dear) appears—
hanging at first, so very low...
*and* underneath its golden glow
the sheep do leap -
ensuring everyone's good sleep.
How they frolic, to and fro -
with a baa, baa, baa
and many leaps so sweet—
the sheep *lull* and *lullaby*...
a busy (tired) world to sleep.

www.ingramcontent.com/pod-product-compliance
Lightning Source LLC
Chambersburg PA
CBHW042141290426
44110CB00002B/80